A Cynic Caught in the Rain

Madison Edwards

A Cynic Caught in the Rain

© 2017 Madison Edwards

Edwards, Madison

1st Edition

ISBN-13: 978-1543072099

ISBN-10: 1543072097

Cover art and foreword by Leah Wood

To contact the author, send an email to madisonvedwards@gmail.com

for the grieving. the afraid. the hopeful. the mentally-ill. the cynics. the ones who feel forgotten.

for my family. with love and a desperate hope we will someday understand one another.

for magical women everywhere. may each of your days be filled with progress, support, and empowerment.

and for my dear husband. your love has given me purpose. you deserve everything in the world and more.

be easy.

take your time.

you are coming

home.

to yourself.

-- Nayyirah Waheed

A Cynic Caught in the Rain

Madison Edwards

Foreword

There are few words that hold enough weight to sink through the depths of my turbulent mind. I find it fascinating that there are bits and pieces of my soul capable of connecting with spilled ink even before I know those feelings are present. This book is a collection of poetry that did just that.

Madison and I met through Twitter several years ago and over the course of the last year and a half, we've become great, close friends. I can't begin to describe how much joy and love she has added to my life. She is brave and passionate and so talented. Her voice is truly honest— something I am trying desperately to master myself. When she asked me to illustrate the cover for this collection of her deepest thoughts, I was so honored and excited.

I remember reading her first draft. I was up late that night because my sick brain wanted to figure the world out instead of finding a place to rest. I rolled off the bed and sat on the floor in the dark reading the document that would become "A Cynic Caught in the Rain."

I sat there, while tears danced along the corners of my eyes, hooked on every word, feeling understood. Feeling safe. Feeling vulnerable and good. Each poem brought up thoughts in me that I had hidden because I was unable to express them properly. It's as if all the toxic air I had held in my lungs could finally be released.

I exhaled and it began to heal me.

Madison provides a space for all people to feel loved. Her words are raw and sharp and bold, as well as filled with the deepest sincerity. This became a space I could acknowledge my trauma and realize that I was not alone. "A Cynic Caught in the Rain" is not only beautifully written, but is also an honest look into very stigmatized, painful realities. I will always be amazed at how effortlessly a raw emotion can become art that facilitates understanding. Madison's voice portrays nothing but goodness and growth in a world that can be so cruel, so evil, and so abusive.

I am so honored to have been included in this written body of work. I will never be able to express my gratitude for writers like Madison who seek to open dialogue between people and who work tirelessly for their words to be a refuge to all in need of one.

I hope you find rest in these words just as I have.

-- Leah Wood, *illustrator and graphic designer*

Introduction

A Cynic Caught in the Rain is a collection of prose and poetry written over a three-year period. Just as the author does when reading, she encourages you to make notes in the margins. Whether you do so by underlining, drawing, or quickly writing whatever floods your mind as you read, know this is a space meant to become yours as well.

Here, grief is welcomed and the outcasts find a home. Here, mental illness loses its stigma and the black sheep gather together. Here, you are seen.

Please, won't you stay awhile?

<u>a wake</u>

I have always been so goddamn afraid for you.

Did you know that when the earth wakes,

you are expected to as well?

It begins with the light, streaming in carefully through the

windows, the blinds, the curtains,

the spaces we forget about.

Sometimes, *we* are spaces we forget about.

This light spills into each dusty corner,

our chosen burial places for the remnants of memories

once living and breathing.

Now you must pay your respects to the dead

and open your weary eyes.

Is this why it's called "a wake"?

Good morning.

You're alive, does it feel like it?

Life has begun again,

and I am so goddamn afraid for you still.

When the flower grows, it is a slow work, an unappreciated work. Tedious? Perhaps. But it is the sort of work photographers enjoy stopping for, if that means anything to you at all. This thing mother earth pushed to the surface, where we walk and create and kill and fight and die, will live forever simply because intrigue captured it in its palms. Pictures will hang in a gallery someday, displaying the immortality of progress. I will die before the fucking plant does.

There is a sort of grace for something that attempts life outside of its womb, as long as it does not speak. The heavy work of existing is praised, if you are a flower. From dirt, it came, and it did not make a mess whilst under the sun. Until its death, of course. Falling apart, slowly, back to its roots. Poor thing, couldn't help it. The petals fell because there was no longer anything to look up for. Death comes for the beautiful as well, isn't that peculiar?

I believe in the souls of flowers. When they die, I feel it. When they are born, I am moved. Few respond so similarly when I emerge and expire, every godforsaken day. Where is my grace? Does progress lose its luster when I open my mouth just like you? If a photographer captured my image just as I bloomed, my picture would be burned. My hair wilts, falls, and tries again. My face is home to blemishes and trails etched from tears, won't you come take a walk sometime? Tattered threads keep me warm, and thankfully so. This world is so goddamn cold. I grow, every single day, I grow. But the camera is uninterested, for grace ends where I begin.

<u>numb</u>

Small circles with my fingers.

Gentle, now. Gentle.

Be patient, like God commands.

But what is patience if I cannot breathe?

I am frantic, frantic and alone.

Must I beg?

Gentle, woman.

But this body is unfamiliar with a loving touch.

I beg.

"Release, feel something again.

We are dying."

It happens suddenly,

but I am not fulfilled.

Am I ever?

There is nothing left for me to give today.

I am unable to love even myself.

There now, lay back.

It's over.

Sleep steals me away while I weep.

"I want to die. I want to die. I want to die."

<u>disadvantage</u>

It's a little bit like waking up while fully submerged. Your eyelids fight against the pressure of the water, and, of course, it is always surprising to wake and find you cannot breathe. There is no gentle way to greet the new day; you're fighting to stay alive before your feet have even hit the floor. So now, your eyes are open and your first thought is *I didn't know I could open my eyes underwater.* And then your lungs are suddenly burning and your feet start kicking and every part of you is screaming to escape the deep waters. But, you can't. The surface doesn't seem to exist and there is no room for adaptation because you are human, and humans do not get easy outs like some optimists would have you believe. Humans only get rocks in their pockets, and while some have been thrown in with their hands free, others find their wrists have been tied together. Whatever energy one had going under has been expelled by trying to stop sinking. Bubbles, rushing to an unattainable surface in a body of water so unforgiving. There is no one here to extend a hand should you need it. This, this is death and I am drowning.

"Love keeps no record of wrongs."

Well, maybe I don't fucking love you then.

preacher man

I have learned to seek refuge in the arms of anyone but you,

for yours hold too tightly,

squeezing the air from my already-tired lungs.

You were there when I emerged from the womb

and you became the first man to hold me,

the first man to falsely assume ownership over my naked body,

setting precedence for the rest.

When you heard my infant cry, did it make you feel something?

Perhaps it affected us both, for I've been crying

in your presence ever since.

I love you is carved into the skin covering your angry hands,

But angry hands still shake

and you've always said sinners cling to their flesh.

<u>she</u>

Tell me, when the womb of a woman kept you alive,

were you so deeply offended by her magic,

the kind you cannot recreate,

you grew into someone devoted

to the oppression of it?

Knock, you said,

and the door will be opened.

So, I knocked.

I knocked every fucking minute

of every fucking day.

I knocked during the night

when the panic attacks woke me up.

I knocked when they told me

depression is a sin.

I knocked even when you went silent.

I knocked

and I knocked

and I knocked.

Now I'm standing at this godforsaken door,

knuckles bleeding,

dry bones showing,

done

waiting for someone

that was never going to come.

<u>women, pt. one</u>

As is true

for Creators,

we always rise again.

They said it was going to be like coming home.

And maybe that's why I couldn't do it.

Maybe that's why I was wary to even pass the threshold.

<u>2:06 am</u>

I'm a little drunk right now on cheap wine, but I think it's good for writing, so here I am. Here we are. I have something to say, but I should say it slowly and meticulously because I mean it, regardless of the empty bottle: you ground me like this floating earth while making me feel as impossible as the stars. I love you. I love you when I'm drunk and I love you when I'm sober. I love you. I love you. I love you. My god, do I love you.

<u>women, pt. two</u>

You cannot silence my voice
and cry out when I bite your hand.
It was not I who drew first blood.

<u>(3) missed calls</u>

The telephone rings

with your name displayed

and I silence it a third time,

so afraid you'll somehow

find a way to

crawl out of the speaker

just to repeat how

disappointed you are in me again.

I hope I drown on all of these goddamn tears.

Dry, empty eyes,

like finding the end of

your whiskey bottle at 2am,

is a fate far worse than death.

The ground is crumbling beneath me

and there is little left to place my feet upon.

Are the walls closing in on you too?

I can't breathe.

It's all falling apart.

Oh my god, it's really falling apart.

I once wrote about faith,

describing it as stepping past the shoreline

into an unknown body of water.

But I realized, as the waves crashed over me

and my lungs fought against a persistent salt water,

I didn't suddenly love swimming

like the haven with a steeple said I would.

Death found me as my body grew weary of seeking.

And as the prayers of many attempted

to resurrect my lifeless body,

I was thankful for the newfound quiet.

I no longer had to work to stay afloat.

I had finally found what the religious spoke of,

a secret, still place

for me to rest in peace.

I don't know how to put it into words that flow well. This beast does not know the kindness of grace, the breath of mercy. It is broken glass on hidden tiles that gets lodged in the calloused skin of your bare feet. It is tea meant to soothe but burns the tongue, leaving you unable to taste, unable to enjoy. It is the first moments of a quiet morning, fuzzy because of the sleepless night before. The sadness suffocates, and the hopelessness demands your attention. Days are shorter, nights are longer. Nothing makes sense but it's familiar, so the welcome mat gets straightened once more, just in case. No, I don't know how to describe what it's like to carry a shadow, just that the weight is always surprising. 'When it rains, it pours,' I whisper with a scorched tongue and sore feet, hardly ready to face another day of surviving.

The pastor read from the holy book,

"Blessed are those who have not seen

and still believed,"

and I swear every goddamn scab

my body has tried to piece back together

tore off in one cruel motion.

Now there is fresh blood

pouring from old wounds

and I'm cursing the words

so many have built their lives on;

feeling cursed myself.

I am haunted by ghosts I invited in,

ghosts who are just as lonely,

ghosts that look so much like me.

I have spent a long time

struggling to put into words

what your absence has done to me.

I still cannot articulate it,

but, my god, I am free now.

You are gone and I am free.

<u>patriarchy</u>

It wasn't you I hated. It was just, the air. Could you tell? It was thicker when you were around. Made it harder for me to breathe. Made it harder for me to be desperate for anything other than an atmosphere that didn't crush me.

<u>woman</u>

I actually think

I don't take up

enough space.

Make room for me,

I am ever-growing

and I am not going to stop

just because

you are not.

intoxicated

He tastes me slowly,

as though I am a fine wine.

Soft lips, appreciative lips,

thirsty lips.

I didn't want to write each of you individual poems

or even acknowledge I still think of you,

this many years later.

But if my eyes close for too long,

I can still feel your wicked hands

wandering past the caution tape

my shirt

my bra

my pants

my trust.

So, here is your fucking poem

about your foreign fingers inside of me

when I begged them not to be;

about your attempts to undress me

while I fought to escape.

I'm told I have PTSD now,

and all you have is this one page in a book.

<u>refugee</u>

Here, our bombs

more commonly detonate

from white tongues

and large wallets.

It will not always be safer

in the land built on genocide,

but, if you are willing,

you could give me your tears,

and I will hold them close.

Follow me home,

take off your shoes,

and know you are welcome here.

Have a seat at the table

where the food is still hot

and a place mat waits for you

always.

What does it feel like to be a writer? God, I don't know. Have you ever stubbed your toe or lost a lover or cut yourself shaving? It feels like intentionally doing all of those things, all at once, all the time. You have to, you know? Being a writer means I have to make myself bleed if I want anything I write to be considered "art." If I want my writing to make people feel something, I have to feel something. We have enough meaningless shit from people who were happy and satisfied when they sat down to create. Paintings of sunsets, sketches of flowers, songs and poems about being in love. Enough, okay? That's not real life, not for the majority of us. I'm not going to open a book of inspirational one-liners and walk away convinced I just experienced what it means to be alive. But, fuck. If I open a book of poetry, written by someone whose blood you can practically trace with your fingertips on each page, that will really mean something. I'm talkin' someone who just walked in on the love of their life in bed with another person, another person who was supposed to be them but wasn't because life is just shit like that. If this human, shocked and hurt and confused and numb, collapsed on the floor and just started scribbling out the only words that came to mind mid-fall and published it in a book, I would buy it, read it, and be changed by it. And that's what I think all writers strive for, you know? Things move us and change us, so we write it all down before tending to the wound and, consequently, people are eventually reading something that once left your heart and didn't come back. Okay, sure, that's a little gruesome. But isn't it also kind of stunning? There is blood being pumped through my body *right now* that will someday drip onto a crumpled piece of paper and give a sort of life to someone else. I can't wrap my head around how profound that is. I can only decide to be a part of it. Life will keep being life, and it's eventually going to fucking drown me. But, until then, you can find me writing madly between all of the breathing and breaking and bleeding. Does that answer your question?

No one needed permission to conceive me,

nor do I need permission to be fully alive.

A love letter to my body

my stretch marks

the dark patches of hair I haven't removed;

to the dry skin on my toes

the scars scattered like stardust

across a galaxy that is breathing and so alive.

You are Good and you are mine,

the only thing I have for sure.

<u>passing time</u>

The End came for me

like she does everyday

and sat quietly as

I drank wine in the dark.

Our breathing,

soft and unbothered,

tangled together,

old friends.

Patiently waiting.

"Not yet," I sigh.

"Maybe tomorrow."

She kisses me before leaving

and I pour myself more wine,

alone again.

i am, pt. one

I am neither present

nor absent.

I am neither awake

nor asleep.

I am neither excited

nor afraid.

I am only waiting

for life to stop

feeling like such

a goddamn chore.

45

You have emboldened

the worst of us.

You have mocked

the very best of us.

You have targeted

the most vulnerable of us.

You have encouraged

the oppression of minorities among us.

You have banned

the most peaceful of us.

You have earned

every bit of

anger

passion

grief

and resistance.

When the people revolt,

we will come for you first

and the rains of justice shall

finally come down.

If we're being honest here,

and I hope we are,

I have always envied the ways

you've all so easily belonged to one another.

After these long years

of growing and leaving and learning to do both,

that bond is still unbroken

and I am still on the outside looking in.

i am, pt. two

I am waiting for sleep.
I am
always
waiting for sleep.

TRAUMA

no pause

break

or period

just an echoing cry for help

from someone who trusted too much

and was burned

by hellfire disguised as holy water

I longed for home

but never did find it

when I returned to

the place of my childhood.

i am, pt. three

I am too much
and not enough.
Growing
learning
changing
regressing
falling
all the time.
It never ends.
I am standing still
and drowning.
I do not know
which is worse.

insult to injury

It will not stop replaying,

the way your knife twisted

counter-clockwise

into my burdened back.

The internal organs

collapsed

so quickly

under grief's weight.

My god and I died together,

but there will be

no resurrection

this time.

<u>genetics</u>

My father was tall, but it was an accident. His family was made up of short men, short women. They never took up much space. Still don't. I think he resented that. He always tried to grow taller. "Wow, you're tall," they'd say. And he would grow another inch before responding, "I know."

My mother was very short, but that was also an accident. She had tall family members, very tall. But she never did like heights or expectations. She shrunk and then tried to teach me how.

But there was a space between my parents, one my dad skipped and one my mother was afraid of. This is where I'm growing now. No accidents. Just what I choose.

Take it.

Hurry,

before this, like everything else,

begins to drift.

Tuck it away.

Remember.

Learn.

Sleep and wake up.

Start again.

Always start again.

broken time, broken company
_____

I know it's been so long

that the clock doesn't even

tell time anymore.

But I didn't mean to shut you out.

I've just been busy

being alive

the only ways I know how;

carefully,

slowly.

Tiptoeing around

open wounds.

Pretty thing,

have you ever been called

anything else?

I will write you a poem

and kiss your hands

and for this one moment,

you will not have to read

between the lines.

I was planted in a pot full of recycled soil

and told to dig deep,

but not too deep,

only where it was comfortable and worn.

But I have never liked small spaces,

always felt somehow threatened by walls.

So I cried and uprooted myself,

after all those stagnant years,

saying sorry, I'm sorry.

The accusations came,

as I suppose they must,

like wild darts.

Traitor.

Outsider.

Disappointment.

The people I loved became

the people I was afraid of.

But I could run now.

The grief took a name, but I don't know what it is because I haven't made the time to get well-acquainted. When it calls, I let it go to a voicemail-box that is too full. When I pass it on the street, I avoid making eye contact by dipping into a store I would never have otherwise been interested in. When it needs a safe place to land, I cross my arms and say, "Not here. God, please not here."

<u>post-mortem</u>

The ghosts of my past, present, and future have gotten together and would like to talk to me. I'm not ready.

But it is so hard to hide from myself.

no vacancy

I cannot be a home for you.

Put your coat back on,

I mean it.

You mustn't stay here.

The floors creak

in the middle of the night

every night

and all the windows are stuck.

It storms so often

and I meet the floods

as they come

rushing through

the tattered roof

I've never learned to patch.

And when the rain finally soaks into

every goddamn corner of me,

I'll spend my hours begging

for a warmth that never comes.

You see, I cannot even be a home for myself.

I cannot even be a home for myself.

<u>mother earth</u>

tears flowing

like the sweet milk

from a mother's breast,

answering the call of life

that is so damn hard today

and yesterday

and probably tomorrow too.

but she has given us

at least one chance.

time keeps passing

but i have yet to,

destined to keep waking up one more day,

one more sunrise,

one more chance to die in

less obvious ways.

<u>they call her the church</u>

Like Christmas for the disobedient child,

I was given handfuls of coal

in exchange for a heart willing

to return to the place of my death.

As the flesh from my hands

burned like Hell,

the congregation rejoiced.

"Holiness is forged in the fire."

Now my hands are scarred like your Christ's

and I stand in the rain any chance I get.

heartbreak

what was once abrupt and dramatic

and like pieces of a window shattering

is now acupuncture,

needles pricking lightly

and gathering

and staying.

it is supposed to heal,

i am supposed to heal,

but there are so many needles now.

I have a sip of water between

drags of my cigarette

so this tired body will not

be thirsty when it's finally time to go.

you taste like the coffee we'll be

drinking when we wake up in the morning;

quiet and inviting,

forgiving.

a relief for the woman who spent her

whole night fighting to survive until

daylight, one more fucking time.

which mug is your favorite?

let me have my coffee in that one.

let me taste you every way i can.

Like stabbing a flag

into an untouched moon,

you declared

my body

yours.

Other explorers would come later,

maybe even remark on the

footprints of those who paved the way,

but you were the first.

I've since burned your flag,

and of course, theirs as well,

to take back what is mine.

But on days like today,

when the sun is hiding

and I'm anxious,

I let myself remember

how it feels to hate you.

i'm told time moves slowly,

but the ticking seems faster

each time i stop to hear it.

"don't. forget. to. live,"

it whispers in hushed, staccato tones.

hiding from whatever is chasing it.

the tempo gets faster

and i feel the fear of

everything catching up.

<u>life cycle</u>

Wild and unruly,

growing quickly along

the walls of that brick

I've always loved,

always pointed out.

Exposed, remember?

Cut down when

I am overgrown,

overly loud,

overstaying my welcome.

But the new buds come

with warmer weather

and we will all

start again.

holy matrimony

I asked to make love and began weeping halfway through

as if something broke inside of me when we came together.

Nothing goes the way we think it should,

not even when the love is deep and kind.

I couldn't stop the tears,

just like I cannot stop the sadness.

And you understood,

said it was okay.

But nothing is okay

and we can't make it through

the delusion of hope and a second chance.

When you slip your fingers inside of me,

I only think of death and the end of all good things.

Your love is truly like a drug,

but not even a good trip can hide us

from our respective graves.

And as for me, well,

I will love you for as long as I can and the best I can,

but if that means holding your magical hands

as we fall six feet under,

will you promise that will be enough?

If it is not enough,

I am so afraid more than a dam will break inside of me.

My cynicism and your faith

are at war with one another.

I didn't mean to turn it into a fight,

but "opposites attract" is a lie.

And your god is so cruel.

And I am so tired.

The air is choking us all.

Every fight feels like the end of the world. The next morning, when it isn't, I try to stop hoping the next night will finish what's been started.

And tonight,

if I carve

twenty-seven more

little bloody lines into

my war-torn thighs,

he will blame himself.

I cannot die without

killing someone else too.

black lives matter and i am so sorry

Watching you die

over and over again

but with a different face

each time,

I find myself wishing

I hadn't spent my entire life

fighting against your resistance,

your determination to exist

as much as I do.

Your bodies have always

littered the boats

the fields

the streets

and I hurried to the sidewalk

with my pale and privileged skin

locking the car doors

to avoid facing you.

There is blood on my hands

from covering the fresh

gunshot wounds in your

chests

stomachs

backs

and my throat is sore

from begging you to stop

bleeding so loudly.

Few things are as

gracious and patient

as the rain falling

early in the morning

making that dripping sound

I love so much,

the one that is simply

droplets hitting earthy divots

beneath my window

but sounds so much like hope.

God, how I've needed a reason

to write about hope.

regret

We both met as so many of us do in the Bible Belt,

hiding in the corners of a church get-together.

I still remember what you were wearing,

the blue white and yellow flowery dress

white high heels

an uncertain smile.

You told me hello and I sighed with relief,

happy the burden of initiating was not on me.

I have never been good at taking steps

unless they are fast and afraid.

We chatted and laughed and talked about

how awkward these things can be.

You told me you were new to this church,

said I looked new too.

I averted my gaze and sheepishly explained that no,

I actually come here every week

and hide in this very corner.

The following Sunday, I was at your house

having lunch with you and your husband.

You made burgers that were a little overdone

but they tasted so kind

and the sweet tea you had brewed seemed

to balance it all out anyways.

I would have asked to do the dishes,

but we ate on paper plates and drank from red solo cups

so I merely gathered up the mess and pushed it down into

the large black bin underneath the sink.

The three of us watched a football game for

a little while afterwards until I finally admitted

I don't particularly like sports.

You laughed and said you didn't either,

but your husband does and there's nothing good on

Sunday television so you don't mind.

I hugged you both

and we made plans for a week from then.

I wish we had kept doing this for longer than

the next three weeks.

I wasn't a vegetarian yet so I didn't mind eating burgers

with your little family every seven days

if it meant I kept feeling safe and fed and loved.

But I wasn't expecting that you wouldn't feel
all of those beautiful things from me.

The preacher had spoken of secret sin just an hour before
and it was convicting enough for the congregation
to start the music back up again and confess
all of their shit to whomever was willing to listen and pray
that their souls would be set free from temptation.
And that's when you pulled me aside, shaking,
ready to admit to me that you were actually a lesbian.
You loved your husband so much,
you were the best of friends,
but the kisses you shared
have never been electric like
those you gave your girlfriend in secret.
And you didn't want me to stop being your friend
but you also knew you couldn't change to
be what this place with its devoted goers wanted.
The tears spilled from your eyes as you explained
you had just talked to the preacher's wife
and she had tried to cast the demons out of you
instead of listening.

I was so stunned and so confused and

all of the words I wish I had said never really came

to the forefront of my mind.

So I just stared blankly at you and backed away a little

before asking if you wanted me to pray

for you to be healed.

I wish these weren't the last words I ever said to you,

but I deserved the way you ran from me.

I was so cruel back then.

The next Sunday, you were not there and I sat by myself

in the back corner once again.

I scanned the crowd slowly,

hoping you would walk through those doors and give

Jesus a chance to set you free from your perversion.

But you never did and missed the preacher's sermon

on how people can be healed from homosexuality since

it is so obviously a choice

and a distortion

of nature,

disgusting in the eyes of God.

I remember thinking, wow, if only you hadn't ran

from the truth.

It has been about four years since you cooked me burgers

and refused to let me sit alone in the back of that church.

And I think of you often.

I hope you are well and surrounded by friends who

do not call you perverted,

but loved.

I hope it has been four years since anyone has tried to

"cure" or cast demons out of you.

And, oh god,

I hope no one has used your life and vulnerability

to build another shame-inducing sermon.

I didn't know it then, but I know it now

that there is nothing unnatural about who you are.

You loved me better than I could love you,

and I am so sorry.

<u>mania</u>

It was like waking up to find
I could see colors I never knew existed;
a golden hour as desperate for me
as I had been for it.
A slowly realized brilliance,
like the orchestra
approaching its collective cue.
One instrument, then three, then ten,
can you hear it?
The percussion's slow crescendo,
something beautiful is about to happen.
They're all taking a breath now
and I am holding mine.
When I begin to wonder
if I will ever breathe again,
this is when maestro
must finally lower his arms.
The song,
oh god, the song
floods my body

with light

and love

and peace

and laughter

and courage

and what

perhaps others

may call

happiness.

I call it

strange.

The notes string together

and I can no longer

find myself;

I no longer need to.

There is no heaven

but this unexpected song.

diagnosis

I've been having trouble sleeping lately

and waking up so early in the morning

for over a week now.

A familiar cycle,

a cruel cycle.

And I'll lay there

waiting for the sun to meet me

looking up "symptoms of bipolar disorder ii"

on my phone because my psychiatrist mentioned it

in passing and I cannot unhear it.

Then I'll spend the next few hours

trying to pretend as though

I didn't see the search engine results.

"Difficulty sleeping.

Waking early."

Denial.

Trying to go back to sleep.

Forever.

Stuck in my head. Stuck in my head. Stuck in my head.
Stuck in my head. Stuck in my head. Stuck in my head.
Stuck in my head. Stuck in my head. Stuck in my head.
Stuck in my head. Stuck in my head. Stuck in my head.
Stuck in my head. Stuck in my head. Stuck in my head.
Stuck in my head. Stuck in my head. Stuck in my head.
Stuck in my head. Stuck in my head. Stuck in my head.
Stuck in my head. Stuck in my head. Stuck in my head.
Stuck in my head. Stuck in my head. Stuck in my head.
Stuck in my head. Stuck in my head. Stuck in my head.
Stuck in my head. Stuck in my head. Stuck in my head.
Stuck in my head. Stuck in my head. Stuck in my head.
Stuck in my head. Stuck in my head. Stuck in my head.
Stuck in my head. Stuck in my head. Stuck in my head.
Stuck in my head. Stuck in my head. Stuck in my head.
Stuck in my head. Stuck in my head. Stuck in my head.
Stuck in my head. Stuck in my head. Stuck in my head.
Stuck in my head. Stuck in my head. Stuck in my head.
Stuck in my head. Stuck in my head. Stuck in my head.
Stuck in my head. Stuck in my head. Stuck in my head.
Stuck in my head. Stuck in my head. Stuck in my head.
Stuck in my head. Stuck in my head. Stuck in my head.
Stuck in my head. Stuck in my head. Stuck in my head.
Stuck in my head. Stuck in my head. Stuck in my head.
Stuck in my head. Stuck in my head. Stuck in my head.
Stuck in my head. Stuck in my head. Stuck in my head.
Stuck in my head. Stuck in my head. Stuck in my head.
Stuck in my head. Stuck in my head. Stuck in my head.
Stuck in my head. Stuck in my head. Stuck in my head.
Stuck in my head. Stuck in my head. Stuck in my head.
Stuck in my head. Stuck in my head. Stuck in my head.
Stuck in my head. Stuck in my head. Stuck in my head.

TW: suicide

I tried to kill myself today,

so you tried to kill yourself too.

By saving me.

By putting yourself between the end

and my grasp.

By telling me to wake up

at least one more time.

You must be so tired.

I know I am.

But, then again,

I did only just wake up.

I know what I am made up of.

Shit like wounds and courage

and anger and passion.

But I cannot be alone,

so, please, save your breath.

My brain,

a ticking time-bomb,

needs a target

and it's usually me.

Defenseless.

Against myself.

psychiatry

He tells me I have a lot of strengths.

I am clearly insightful.

I will make it through.

With the right medications,

frequent therapy,

I will someday find I can thrive.

But I can't yet

and today was longer than yesterday.

I keep forgetting to take my morning meds

because I am used to taking them

before I fall asleep at night.

And the appointments are all so expensive.

I don't make enough money

to treat my fucked up brain.

And, eventually, I'll quit my job

because I cannot handle keeping one

for more than a few months.

When I interview for the next one,

they'll point that out,

like they always do.

And I'll make up some sort of excuse,

already planning another escape route.

Besides, he used the word "thrive,"

as though I'd understand what it meant.

I don't.

I don't think I ever have.

My hands are shaking now,

and my mind is wandering

to literally anything else.

Avoidance as a mental illness symptom.

Obsession as another.

Fear, for when I get bored.

You'll have to learn how to

compromise with yourself

or you will be miserable

your whole life.

I should know.

I think I have been miserable

my whole life.

I do not feel brave

for writing the things

I cannot say out loud.

Sometimes,

even the truth feels like hiding.

If the only poem you can wring

from your tired, aching fingers

is one of the pain of living

in a world dying quickly

with people who are cruel and greedy,

you should still squeeze out

every

last

drop.

As, of course,

this life will do to us.

Duet

Loving you,

dearest,

is perhaps

the only good thing

I know how to do.

My pain, though vast,

will always find

small silver linings

amid the work of your lungs.

And when it gets too hard,

don't be afraid of rest.

Take my hand

and we'll retire

from life's labors

together.

I dreamt of cutting the pink out
of my hair and woke up crying,
grieving the loss of the first thing
I ever did for myself.

Where do I go when there's nothing left for me here?

Is there no refuge for us prodigal children

fleeing home to write a story of our own,

a narrative in which we don't return?

I'm desperate to make a safe place

we never must leave

to begin with.

mantra

May we be mindful

of ourselves and others,

of each breath we can

either give or take.

May we be mindful

of how mother earth feels

below us, above us,

and within us.

May we be mindful

and free to exist

right now, right here,

right in the middle of it all.

May we be mindful

of this magic,

an audience captivated

by the experience.

May we be mindful

of deep suffering,

abrupt endings,

the absence of kindness and justice.

May we be mindful

and unafraid to advocate for,

fight against,

and usher in all things Good.

May we be mindful,

may we be fierce,

and may we be caretakers

before we are anything else.

I hope to someday

nourish the earth

like she has

nourished me.

exclusion

The thing I hate most of that monotheistic religion,

and there are so many things I hate about it,

is the promise of new life to the most trusting of us.

And I suppose new life was also given to the skeptics,

but it just wasn't the same.

Skeptics, already suspicious from life fucking them over,

received new life in the form of ebb and flow.

The questions ebbed like a tide when they begged for sleep,

and their dreams flowed with scenes from hell.

To trust is so hard, but the alternative is fear.

The privileged, the naïve, are not afraid.

They do not know any better.

When that holy book demands hearts full of peace,

its followers sink into the bliss of ignorance,

and the rest of us follow the tide until

we are so far away.

Does growing ever look like cynicism?

God, I hope so.

I'm just scared, I suppose,

I'll get caught in the rain and rediscover

a taste of endurance.

And it will keep me going for

the rest of today,

like it sometimes does.

But tomorrow is still coming.

And I don't think it's supposed

to rain then.

I used to love the rain, too.

I'm not sure why anymore.

I don't know what it may look like to thrive someday,

but I am afraid it will erase the bits and pieces of me

I've been clutching so terribly close to my patchwork chest.

I don't want to lose me.

I don't want to lose me.

I don't want to lose me.

I have lost everything else.

Please, I don't want to lose me.

a confessional

When the skies open wide
and Mother begins to cry,
I lift these wicked hands
to join the chorus.
The buds of the earth grow taller
as the rest of us bend
under the weight of grief's showers.
She has carried us for so long,
but we are getting so heavy.
We are getting so selfish.
The flowers are beautiful,
but we've stepped on those too.

The sun?

Oh, it will probably rise again.

If you find you feel forgotten,

and I'm sorry to say so many of us do,

know there is still a solace to be found,

for *you've* taken the time to remember yourself

and that is how we all begin to heal.

I suppose it was the smell of honey-suckle

being pollinated by a hundred bees

that reminded me life

is sometimes

worth living.

<u>reborn</u>

And I'm waking up
the slumbering giant within me,
the one who learned to survive
when it stopped making sense to.

Today might be easier.
I cannot know for sure,
but the sky is weeping
instead of me.

I am the cynic

and the rain,

caught in every version of myself.

And when the storm finally breaks,

weary from the previous night of sorrow,

I hope you'll think kindly of me

and look upon the quiet morning

with understanding eyes.

Acknowledgements

Evan James, for loving me and showing up for me, especially when I was unable to do so for either one of us. Thank you for supporting my dreams and teaching me to trust my voice. Thank you for your input and for treating each word I write as something important and Good. I love you so deeply, so desperately.

Leah, for illustrating the stunning cover, which helped bring this entire collection to life. Additionally, for writing the foreword and filling it with your kindness. For your friendship, for your willingness to be an important part of my life, for being the embodiment of goodness, graciousness, fairness, love, and advocacy, I give all of my thanks and love.

#CoolGirlsontheInternet, for welcoming me in when I had no one else; for loving me, supporting me, and teaching me to be brave and fierce like yourselves.

Lakisha, for providing a safe place for me to grieve, learn, heal, move forward, and grow.

Joe van Gogh family, for making space for me to join such a stellar group of people. You've accepted me, exactly as I am, from the beginning.

The family I married into, for loving me immediately and wholly, regardless of the ways I differed from you.

My immediate family, for loving me steadfastly and teaching me the value of devoting oneself to things that give and encourage life; for opening yourselves to learning how to appreciate who I am ever-becoming.

And finally, *all others who have listened to me, followed me, supported me, accepted me,* you are the reason I've found the courage to publish anything at all. Thank you and namaste.

About the Author

Madison Edwards is a Texas-born poet and writer based in Durham, North Carolina. Born in 1995, she primarily writes about her experiences with mental illness, trauma, the loss of religious faith, grief, and rebirthing oneself. Madison is newly-married to her husband, Evan, and currently works as a barista while she finishes her degree in Human Services and Social Work.

A Cynic Caught in the Rain is Madison's first published work. You can find her on:

Instagram at @madisonvedwards

Made in the USA
Lexington, KY
21 June 2017